Learn Python
in a
Snap!

1st edition

Rapid introduction to Python for those who
already know Snap! Programming

Abhay B. Joshi

Book series on "Learning computer programming and CS principles"

In memory of Rashmi Pethe, my mother-in-law

Published by:
SPARK Institute and Publications
16668 NE 121st Street
Redmond, WA 98052, USA
1st edition: 15 April 2021

Cover design by:
Ravindra Pande (panravi@yahoo.com)

To order:
Digital (Kindle) version available worldwide on Amazon.com.
Print version available in select countries on Amazon.com.

Other books in this series:
http://www.abhayjoshi.net/spark/csseries.pdf

Preface

Background

I started my CS teaching career with **Scratch**. (Actually, it was with **Logo** and **Alice** but that would be going too far back!) Eventually I faced the question "What after **Scratch**?" Initially it was the parents of my students who posed this question – unfortunately out of ignorance about **Scratch's** capability. Later, I faced the question myself because some of my students had actually done all they could with **Scratch**. In spite of heavy pressure from the **Python** fans, I wasn't convinced that an industry-strength language such as **Python** was a logical next step after **Scratch**. My hesitation was born out of experience – I found that most of my students, who were by then quite comfortable with computational thinking with **Scratch**, struggled with **Python**.

Fortunately, just then, I discovered **Snap!** – a substantial upgrade to **Scratch** and an excellent bridge to **Python**. **Snap** (henceforth stripped of the '!') adds a lot of CS concepts and programming features that are missing in **Scratch**. The continuation of the familiar block-based interface helps students work with these advanced ideas fairly comfortably. In fact, TEALS (a US-based non-profit) has designed a one-year course for high school students that consists of a semester with **Snap** followed by a semester with **Python**! My hunch that **Snap** is an excellent bridge between **Scratch** and **Python** was thus validated.

About this book

In this book, I assume that the reader is intimately familiar with the **Snap** programming language. I simply take **Snap** concepts and features and show their equivalent in **Python**. Since it is assumed that students already understand each concept (for example, 'what is simple looping?') I do not bother to go into the theory but go straight to the **Python** syntax.

In short, this book is for students who are qualified **Snap** *programmers and are looking for a jumpstart into the* **Python** *universe.*

The book is by no means a comprehensive guide to **Python**. It only covers those **Python** features for which an equivalent exists in **Snap**.

How the book is organized

The book is organized as a series of concepts – each explaining a **Snap** concept and its equivalent in **Python**. Ample code examples are provided to elucidate each concept. There are a few programming assignments at the end of the book which try to apply all our learning to a meaningful practice of **Python** programming.

Hardware and Software

This book has been written for **Snap** version 5 and **Python** 3.

Snap is available online at http://snap.berkeley.edu and you can download **Python** 3 from www.python.org.

The program files of all Practice Programs in this book are available as a ZIP file: http://www.abhayjoshi.net/spark/python/book1/files.zip.

Acknowledgements

Most of the material used for this book came from my teaching experience since 2008. I would like to thank TEALS for allowing me to teach **Snap** and **Python** to their students for the last several years. Next, I must thank all my students. They tolerated my ideas, contributed their own, and frankly told me what was interesting and what wasn't. Their projects were amazingly creative – which only reinforced my belief that teaching programming is a good idea!

This book would not have been possible without the constant encouragement of my friends and family.

I do hope that readers will find this book useful and enjoyable.

Abhay B. Joshi (abjoshi@yahoo.com)
Seattle, USA
15 April 2021

Author's background

As a freelance teacher (since 2008), Abhay's area of interest has been "teaching Computer Programming as a medium for learning" and he has been teaching Snap, Python, and Scratch regularly to middle and high school students – currently in the Pacific Northwest of USA and Pune, India.

Since 2011 Abhay has authored several books for a series aimed at Learning computer programming and CS principles. He now has sets of 3 books each on **Scratch** and **Snap** Programming which anyone can use to start from the basics and become an expert **Scratch/Snap** programmer. He has also written books on Logo Programming – the granddaddy of and inspiration behind most modern languages meant for CS education. Abhay has written several articles to promote CS education and has conducted teacher-training workshops to encourage aspiring teachers to experiment with this idea.

Abhay has been associated with the Software Industry since 1988 as a programmer, developer, entrepreneur, coach, and adviser. After getting an MS in Computer Engineering from Syracuse University (USA), he worked as a programmer for product companies that developed secure operating systems and network protocols. In 1997, Abhay co-founded Disha Technologies, a successful software services organization.

Programming remains one of Abhay's favorite hobbies, and he continues to explore the "entertaining, intellectual, and educational" aspects of programming.

Author's CS page: http://www.abhayjoshi.net/spark/home.htm

Contents

Learn Python in a Snap!

Getting Started

Dear **Snap** programmer, welcome to the world of **Python**! In this section we will cover the basics of **Python** so that the subsequent sections will become a breeze for you.

Setting up:

I hope you have already downloaded **Python** or decided which environment to use for your purpose. I recommend the IDLE app available at www.python.org as a good beginner's environment. I also hope you have taken the trouble to understand how to use this environment to create your own **Python** projects. There is plenty of documentation provided by all tool suppliers.

If you can type and run the following short program, your setup is working!

```
print( "Welcome to Python!" )
print( "Did you know 2 plus 2 is", 4, "?" )
```

Observations:

The first thing you will notice about **Python** is that it is not a block-based language like **Snap**. There is no drag-and-drop, no graphical interface, and no sprites. **Python** is a text-based language in which you must type all your programs.

Here is an example:

This same script converted to **Python** would appear as follows. You will probably be able to correlate to the script above line by line. Don't worry if you do not understand every line and command, we are going to learn all of it in later sections.

```python
print( "Hello there! Welcome to Snap!" )
name = input( "What's your name? " )
print( name + ", give me two numbers to multiply." )
x = int(input( "Enter the first number: " ))
y = int(input( "Enter the second number: " ))
print( "The product of " + str(x) + " and " + str(y) + " is: " + str(x*y) )
```

Type this script in your **Python** file and run it. Do you see the same behavior as the **Snap** program? The point about "having to type everything" should be clear.

The other thing you will notice is that there are no sprites, so there is no question of multiple sprites communicating using broadcasting. Your **Python** program will be a lot like having a single sprite, without any visual, graphical appearance.

Okay, let us now start learning **Python** features based on our knowledge of **Snap**. You will find that most of your **Snap** expertise transfers nicely to **Python**. I have provided a few practice programs after all concepts are discussed. In addition, you could try to port some of your **Snap** programs to **Python** or look up practice assignments on Internet sites such as codingbat.com.

Section I

CS Concepts

Display Text

In **Snap** we display text (strings) to the user using the 'say' block:

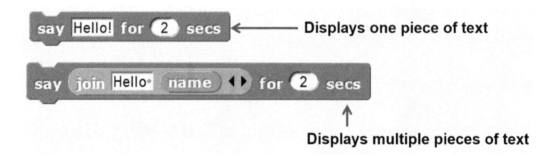

say Hello! for 2 secs ←——— **Displays one piece of text**

say join Hello name ◀▶ for 2 secs

↑
Displays multiple pieces of text

As shown, we use the 'join' operator to combine multiple strings into a single sentence.

We can achieve this functionality in **Python** as shown below:

```
print ( "Hello world!" )
```
←——— **Displays one piece of text**

```
print ( "Hello", name )
```

↑
Displays multiple pieces of text

There are actually two ways in **Python** to concatenate multiple strings. See the example below. (Note: Lines starting with '#' are treated as comments in **Python**).

```
#Using multiple parameters to print
name = "Tony"
print ( "Welcome to Python", name )
```

This will display "Welcome to Python Tony".

```
#Using the + operator
name = "Tony"
print( "Welcome to Python " + name )
```

This will also display "Welcome to Python Tony".

Note that, in the first approach, a space was inserted automatically. The second approach connects strings exactly the way they are.

The first approach has another benefit: it can take other data types (such as integer), whereas in the latter approach you must supply only strings. In the example below, the '+' operator requires that we convert 10 into a string using the str() function.

```
print( "My age is", 10 )
print( "My age is " + str(10) )
```

The print() function is the primary way to display text in **Python**, and it is quite versatile. Here are a few interesting capabilities of print():

Instead of a space character, you can get a different separator character:
```
print( 1, 2, 3, 4, sep=":" )
```

This will display "1:2:3:4".

print() puts a newline ('\n') character at the end. This can also be changed:
```
print( "Welcome to Python!", end=" $$ " )
print( "It is a fun language." )
```

This will produce:
```
Welcome to Python! $$ It is a fun language.
```

Variables

In **Snap** using variables is straightforward. You first create a variable and manipulate it using the 'set' and 'change' commands. See below:

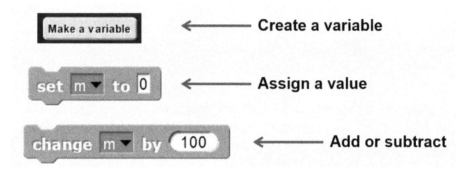

In **Python**, a variable is created (defined) as soon as it appears for the first time on the LHS (left hand side) of an assignment statement. See equivalent **Python** commands below:

$$m = 0 \quad \longleftarrow \textbf{Create variable and assign a value}$$

$$m = m + 100 \quad \longleftarrow \textbf{Add or subtract}$$

Using variables:

Once you create variables, you can use them to create complex expressions. For example, we calculate the hypotenuse of a right-angle triangle using the Pythagorean formula:

Equivalent in **Python**:

```
import math

x = 12
y = 5
z = math.sqrt( x**2 + y**2 )
```

Note the 'import' statement: it is required to import the math library for the sqrt function. Advanced math functions such as sqrt are not part of core **Python**.

Variables can similarly be used as input to any **Snap** block or as arguments to a custom block, as shown below. "Greeting" is a custom block.

Equivalent in **Python**:

```
user = "Tony"
Greeting( user )
```

"Greeting" is a function that you need to define in your **Python** program. (We will learn how to define functions later.)

Naming conventions:

As in **Snap**, case is important in **Python**. That is, for example, variables 'name' and 'NAME' would be treated as two separate variables. But, unlike **Snap, Python** requires that your variable name be a single word – without any space characters. A variable such as the one shown below won't be allowed in **Python**.

Variable scope:

In **Snap**, there are 3 different scopes possible for a variable. If you create a variable that is for "all sprites", it is a "global" variable, which means it is visible to all scripts in the program. If you create a variable that is for "this sprite only", it becomes a "sprite-local" variable, which means it is visible to all scripts of this sprite only. Finally, if you create a variable using the "script variable" block (see example below) it is a "script-local" variable, which means it is only visible to that script or custom block.

```
when space key pressed
script variables (a) ▶
set a to pick random (-100) to (100)
```

'a' is a script-local variable.

```
+ EvenRandom +
script variables (x) ▶
set x to (2) × pick random (-100) to (100)
report x
```

In this custom block, 'x' is a script-local variable.

In **Python**, there are only 2 scopes possible for a variable. When you define a variable outside any function, it is "global" in scope. Variables defined inside a function are "local" in scope, i.e., they are visible only to that function.

In the code below, e1, e2, and h are global variables, and z is a local variable of 'hypotenuse()'.

```python
import math

def hypotenuse( x, y ):
    z = math.sqrt( x**2 + y**2 )
    return z

e1 = 12
e2 = 5
h = hypotenuse( e1, e2 )
print(h)
```

Tips about variable scope:

Since **Python** allows you to define variables on the fly (there is no separate "create" step like in **Snap**) it is easy to confuse global and local variables. For example, if you have a global called 'Score' and inside a function you have:

```python
def myFunction():
    Score = 100
```

Python creates a local variable called 'Score' instead of using the global. If you want to use the global variable, you must have an explicit declaration:

```python
def myFunction():
    global Score
    Score = 100
```

User Input

In **Snap** we get text input from the user using the 'ask' block:

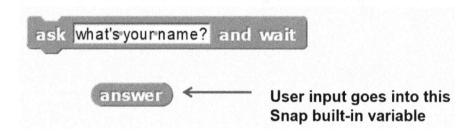

User input goes into this
Snap built-in variable

In **Python**, we use the following trick to achieve the same effect:

```
name = input("What's your name?")
```

User input goes into your own variable.
Note: The input is always in "string" format.

As noted, the input is always a "string" data type. If you are expecting something else – an integer for example – you must apply the appropriate converter function. See the example below. It converts temperature in Celsius to Fahrenheit. We expect an integer input which is provided by the "int" function.

```
celsius = int( input("Enter temperature in celsius: ") )
fahrenheit = (celsius * 9/5) + 32
print( "Temperature in fahrenheit: ", fahrenheit )
```

Similarly, if you are expecting a decimal number (e.g. 10.5), you can use 'float()' to convert from string to float.

There is one difference between how **Snap** and **Python** treat string input. **Snap** is case-insensitive. For example, "john" and "JOHN" are treated the same. **Python** is *case-sensitive*. This can cause a lot of trouble while processing user input. One trick is to always convert user input to lower or upper case, before processing it further. See example below:

```
name = input( "Enter your name: ")
nameLower = name.lower()
```

The function `lower()` converts strings to lower case.

If you don't like having multiple variables for the same thing, you can use the following compact form:

```
name = input( "Enter your name: ").lower()
```

Functions and the dot notation:

Certain **Python** functions, such as `len()` (which gives the length of a given string), are general functions and are accessible directly. And functions like `lower()` are "class methods" which are only accessible through their "class objects", which is when you have to use the dot notation.

```
s = "Hello World"
l = len( s )
ss = s.lower()
```

There is no magic formula to this, and you just need to know which functions are general and which are class methods.

Dot notation is also used for functions that are part of external libraries. In an earlier section we used the 'sqrt' function from the math library using dot notation.

Relational Operators

In **Snap** you can compare two quantities using the following relational operators:

The example shows comparison between variable m and the number 100.

We can do similar comparison in **Python** as follows:

$$m == 100$$

$$m > 100$$

$$m < 100$$

It is important to note that comparison for equality in **Python** requires two '=' signs. The statement m = 100 would be taken as a variable assignment (similar to the 'set' command in **Snap**). Fortunately, **Python** complains if you make such an error in your conditional statements.

String comparison:

Similar to **Snap**, you can compare strings for equality in **Python** also.

`name = Kimble`

Equivalent in **Python**:

```
name == "Kimble"
```

As mentioned earlier (in the "User input" section), string comparisons in **Snap** are not case-sensitive, but in **Python** they are case-sensitive. So, `name = KIMBLE` and `name = Kimble` would both return the same result, but **Python** would expect exact match including case to return True.

Complex comparisons:

We can do additional, a bit more complex comparisons in **Snap** using the Boolean operators. **Python** doesn't require these Boolean operators. The following table shows these comparisons in **Snap** and their equivalent in **Python**:

Snap	Python
`not  m = 100`	`m != 100`
`m < 100  or  m = 100`	`m <= 100`
`m > 100  or  m = 100`	`m >= 100`

Of course, all these comparisons are to be used in conditional statements, such as, IF, about which we will learn soon.

The IF Statement

In **Snap** the conditional IF statement is provided by the block shown below:

The same effect can be achieved in **Python** using the IF block statement:

```python
if (m < n):
    print("m is smaller than n")
    m = n + 100
```

Note the ':' character which indicates the beginning of the command block. Also note the indentation of every line: this must be uniform, because that is how **Python** knows which statements are part of the IF block.

Unlike **Snap**, there is no clearly visible means in **Python** to know where the IF block ends. The only way is to watch the indentation, which can sometimes be tricky. I recommend using a much more visible technique as shown below:

```python
if (m < n):
    print("m is smaller than n")
    m = n + 100
#end if
```

The last line is a **Python** comment and hence is ignored, but it highlights where the IF block ends.

All **Python** block statements (about which we will learn in this book) have this issue of indentation. The slightly complex code sample below demonstrates the utility of this idea of using comments to indicate the end of block statements:

```python
while (True):
    userInput = input( "What do you want to do? " )
    if (userInput == 'help'):
        printHelp()
    #end if
    if (userInput == 'play'):
        playGame()
    #end if
#end while
```

If the command block following the IF statement contains a single instruction, you can put it right after the ':' character. See the example below:

```python
if (a > 0): print( "It is a positive number." )
```

Using IF to check membership:

Python allows IF command to be used to check if an item is a member of an iterable data type (such as a string or a list).

Here is a string example:
```python
str = "this is an example"
if 'this' in str:
    print( "True" )
```

Here is a list example:
```python
L = [5, 10, 40, -90]
if 40 in L:
    print( "True" )
```

The IF-Else Statement

In **Snap** the conditional IF-Else feature is provided by the block shown below:

The same effect can be achieved in **Python** as shown below:

```python
if (m < n):
    print("m is smaller than n")
    m = n + 100
else:
    print("m is not smaller than n")
    m = n - 100
```

There are two command blocks (groups): one for If and the other for Else. Note again the ':' character which indicates the beginning of each command block. Also note the uniform indentation of lines inside each block.

Once again, it is helpful – although not required – to visually indicate where the entire IF-Else statement ends.

```python
if (m < n):
    print("m is smaller than n")
    m = n + 100
else:
    m = n - 100
#end if
```

Nested IF blocks:

Just like in **Snap**, we can have nested IF blocks in **Python**. Here is an example that checks eligibility to run for President:

Equivalent in Python:
```python
age = int( input("What is your age? ") )
if (age > 35):
    born = input("Were you born in the United States? ").lower()
    if (born == "yes"):
        print( "You are eligible to run for President." )
    else:
        print( "Only naturally born citizens are eligible." )
    #end if
else:
    print( "You need to be 35 or older." )
#end if
```

Conditional Expression

Snap offers an interesting feature to create a conditional expression, which can then be used in an assignment statement, to pass arguments to functions, as a return value, or really for any other purpose that allows expressions.

Here is the block that allows conditional expression:

Here is how it can be used in an assignment instruction:

Depending on the value of y, x will get 50 or -50.

Python offers a very similar mechanism. The code below demonstrates an equivalent assignment statement:

```
x = 50 if (y == 0) else -50
```

Just like in **Snap** the conditional expression in **Python** can be used elsewhere too, such as, to pass as an argument to a function, or as a return value.

Here is an example. The function below returns the bigger number of the two.

```
def bigger( x, y ):
    return x if x > y else y
```

The IF-Elseif-Else Statement

Snap does not have an Elseif block, but it can be simulated by a combination of Else and IF-Else as shown below:

Python does have an Else-if construct (it's called elif). The same effect as above can be achieved in **Python** as shown below:

```python
if (m < 0):
    print( "m is negative" )
elif (m > 0):
    print( "m is positive" )
else:
    print( "m must be zero" )
#end if
```

Note that, it is 'elif' and not 'elseif'. Also note the ':' character which is required to indicate the start of every block.

The if-elif-else construct is especially useful when you are dealing with a number of choices. Here is an example: Let's say we are assigning grades to students based on their marks as per the following table:

Marks	Grade
Between 91 and 100	A
Between 81 and 91	B
Between 71 and 81	C
Between 61 and 71	D
Less than 61	F

```
if (marks >= 91 and marks <= 100):
    grade = 'A'
elif (marks >= 81 and marks < 91):
    grade = 'B'
elif (marks >= 71 and marks < 81):
    grade = 'C'
elif (marks >= 61 and marks < 71):
    grade = 'D'
else:
    grade = 'F'
#end if
```

We will learn about Boolean operators such as 'and' above in a following section.

Boolean Operators

Boolean operators, as you know, are for creating compound expressions of conditions. Conditions, i.e. questions that return yes/no or true/false, can be combined using these logic operators.

The basic Boolean operators in **Snap** are:

The last two, as you know, are constants – typically used as return values.

Python offers similar Boolean operators and constants:

```
and
or
not
True
False
```

Here are a few examples of **Snap** Boolean expressions and their **Python** equivalents:

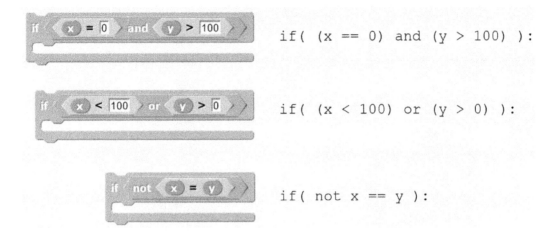

```
if( (x == 0) and (y > 100) ):
```

```
if( (x < 100) or (y > 0) ):
```

```
if( not x == y ):
```

Above, the Boolean expressions are used inside the IF command, but they can used by any command that takes conditional expressions. See the example below in which the "game loop" exits only when gameOver becomes True.

```
gameOver = False
while (not gameOver):
    < game code >
```

You can usually intuitively decide which Boolean operator to use – AND or OR – by looking at how the conditions work together. Here are tips on how to decide:

When you see a nested IF, you can think of AND. The following are equivalent.

```
if (t > 100):
    if (h > 90):
        print( "It's bad!" )
```
⬌
```
if ( (t > 100) and (h > 90) ):
    print( "It's bad!" )
```

When you see multiple blocks of identical code, you can consider using OR:

```
if (userInput == 'h'):
    printHelp()
if (newGame == True):
    printHelp()
```
⬌
```
if (userInput == 'h' or newGame):
    printHelp()
```

Simple Looping

In **Snap** there are two blocks that provide simple looping:

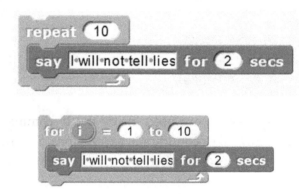

Both the scripts are identical in functionality. The 'for' loop varies i from 1 to 10 (both included).

Python does not have anything like 'repeat' but offers an equivalent of the 'for' loop:

```
for i in range(1, 11):
    print( "I will not tell lies" )
```

The **Python** for loop varies i from 1 to 10 (1 less than the "end value").

The range operator:

The 'range' operator in **Python** is quite versatile. It can take from 1 to 3 inputs: starting value, ending value, step.

If there is only one input, it specifies the 'end value'. The 'starting value' and 'step' inputs are assumed to be 0 and 1 respectively. As a result, in the loop below, i will vary from 0 to 9 resulting in 10 iterations.

```
for i in range(10):
    print( "I will not tell lies" )
```

The 2-input format specifies start/end values. The step input is assumed to be 1. As a result, in the loop below, i will vary from 5 to 14 resulting in 10 iterations.

```
for i in range(5, 15):
    print( "I will not tell lies" )
```

The 3-input format specifies all inputs. As a result, in the loop below, i will vary from 200 to 110 in steps of -10 (200, 190, 180, …, 110) resulting in 10 iterations.

```
for i in range(200, 100, -10):
    print( "I will not tell lies" )
```

Looping for iterable objects:

Python has several data types, such as, string, list, tuple, etc., that are known as 'iterable' data types because they all contain a sequence of items. The FOR loop can be used to enumerate any iterable data type. In this format, the 'range' operator is not used.

The following loop will print a, b, c, d, e one by one.

```
for ch in "abcde":
    print (ch)
```

This idea works similarly for lists, tuples and even files.

Premature loop termination:

You can break out of a FOR loop using the 'break' statement. The loop below will print a and b and then stop because 1 is a digit.

```
for c in "ab1de":
    if c.isdigit(): break
    print (c)
```

Conditional Looping

In **Snap** the 'repeat until' block provides conditional looping:

In the above script, the code inside 'repeat until' runs until n becomes greater than 10. In other words, the inside code runs as long as n <= 10.

Python offers conditional looping in a complementary avatar:

```
n = 1
while (n <= 10):
    print( n, ": I will not tell lies" )
    n = n + 1
```

This code is equivalent to the earlier **Snap** code. The instructions inside the 'while' block run as long as n <= 10. Once again, note the ':' character that is required for all block statements in **Python**. Also note the uniform indentation of all instructions within the 'while' block. These are unique requirements of **Python** programming.

Continue and Break:

Similar to the 'for' loop, you can terminate the 'while' loop using the 'break' statement.

In the example below, imagine that the variable 'error' keeps track of any unforeseen error in the game. If it becomes True, we do not want to continue to game loop any longer. This is accomplished by the 'break' statement.

```
while (not gameOver):
    <game code>
    if (error == True):
        break
```

The 'continue' statement allows you to skip portion of your code. In the example below, we skip all even numbers using 'continue'.

```
y = 10
while (y > 0):
    y -= 1
    if (y % 2 == 0):
        continue
    print (y)
```

Single-line while:

In those rare circumstances in which you have only one instruction inside the while block, you can put it immediately after the ':' character. In the example below, we want the user to enter a positive integer.

```
ui = '0'
while (int(ui) <= 0): ui = input( "Enter a positive integer: ")
```

The forever loop:

Interestingly, you can recreate the effect of the 'forever' **Snap** block using the 'while' construct:

```
while (True):
```

New (custom) Procedures

In **Snap** we can create our own custom procedures (blocks). The following custom block takes one input and has no return value.

Equivalent code in **Python** for this custom block would be called a "function":

```
def Greet( person ):
    print( "Hello", person )
    print( "Welcome to Python" )
```

Note the **uniform indentation** of all instructions inside the function.

Although it is not required, it is a good idea to visually indicate where the function definition ends using a comment line:

```
def Greet( person ):
    print( "Hello", person )
    print( "Welcome to Python" )
#end def
```

A function definition is also a block statement in **Python** (similar to `if`, `for`, `while`, etc.) and hence the ':' character and uniform indentation are mandatory.

Once defined, you can use the new function in your program:

```
name = input( "What is your name? " )
Greet( name )
```

The following **Snap** procedure takes inputs and has a return value as well:

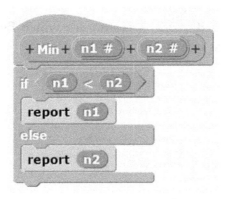

Equivalent procedure (aka function) in **Python** would appear as below:

```
def Min( n1, n2 ):
    if (n1 < n2):
        return n1
    else:
        return n2:
    #end if
#end def
```

Note that the comment lines (starting with '#') are not required but are recommended for better readability.

The following code shows how this function can be used.

```
a = int( input( "Enter a number: " ) )
b = int( input( "Enter a number: " ) )
c = Min( a, b )
print( c, "is the smaller number." )
```

Arithmetic Operators

Snap provides a set of arithmetic operators for which **Python** provides its own equivalents. See the table below:

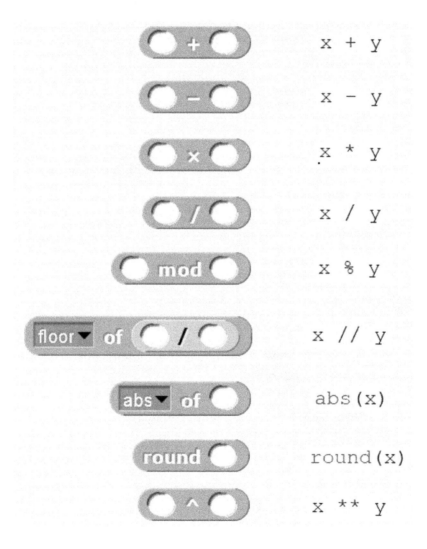

+	x + y
–	x - y
×	x * y
/	x / y
mod	x % y
floor of /	x // y
abs of	abs(x)
round	round(x)
^	x ** y

You are familiar with all the above **Snap** operators, but here are a few quick notes on some of them and their **Python** friends:

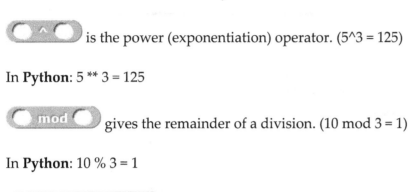 is the power (exponentiation) operator. (5^3 = 125)

In **Python**: 5 ** 3 = 125

gives the remainder of a division. (10 mod 3 = 1)

In **Python**: 10 % 3 = 1

gives integer division. (floor 10/3 = 3)

In **Python**: 10 // 3 = 3

The round() function in **Python** is more versatile than the one in **Snap**. It can take 1 or 2 inputs. With one input, it rounds it to the nearest whole number. With 2 inputs, the 2nd input determines the precision, i.e., how many decimal places the number should be rounded to. See the examples below:

```
print( round(10.7) )
```
⟶ Will display 11

```
print( round(10.673, 2) )
```
⟶ Will display 10.67

There is a whole bunch of additional math operations, such as, trigonometric and logarithmic functions, available in **Python** through its "math" library.

String Operations

Snap provides the following operators to manipulate strings (sequence of alphanumeric characters). In **Python** every string is enclosed in double or single quotes (e.g. "Hello" or 'Hello').

Concatenation:

Snap provides the 'join' operator to connect multiple strings.

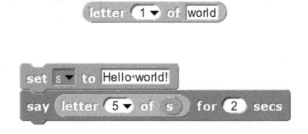

The pop-up bubble shows the output (assuming variable name contains 'Don').

You can do the same thing in **Python** using the '+' operator:

```
"Hello" + name + ", How are you?"
```

The letter operator:

Snap allows you to fetch any letter in a given string using the 'letter' operator.

After running this script, you would see 'o' on the screen.

Doing this in **Python** is a piece of cake. You can simply use the square bracket notation.

```
s = "Hello world!"
print( s[4] )
```

Note an important difference: In **Snap**, we count positions from 1. In **Python** the counting starts from 0. So, 0 gives the first letter, 1 gives the second letter, and so on.

The length operator:

You can find out the length of a string in **Snap** using the 'length' operator:

```
length of text ▢
```

The following script will display 12 on the screen.

```
set s ▾ to Hello world!
say length of text s    for 2 secs
```

Python offers the function len() to get the length of a string.

```
s = "Hello world!"
print( len(s) )
```

Split into substrings:

The 'split' operator lets you split a long string into multiple sub-strings. It returns the sub-strings in a list format.

In **Python**, interestingly, the string data type comes with a `split()` method for the same purpose, which also returns the sub-strings in a list format.

The drop-down list in the above **Snap** block shows different ways in which you can split.

Split into words:

As you can guess, the variable 'ss' will contain a list of 8 words.

This is how you can do this in **Python**:

```
s = "how many words are there in this line?"
ss = s.split()
```

After running this script, the variable 'ss' will contain a list of 8 words:

```
['how', 'many', 'words', 'are', 'there', 'in', 'this', 'line?']
```

Split into letters:

As you can guess, the variable 'ss' will contain a list of 11 letters.

To do this in **Python** we can't use the `split()` function. Instead, we use the casting function `list()`. Casting is a way to convert from one data type to another.

```
s = "hello world"
ss = list(s)
```

After running this script, the variable 'ss' will contain a list of 11 letters:

```
['h', 'e', 'l', 'l', 'o', ' ', 'w', 'o', 'r', 'l', 'd']
```

Splitting into lines:

You can paste an entire text file into a **Snap** string variable and split it into a list of lines. For example, let us paste the following 3 lines into the variable s.

```
This is line 1.
This is line 2.
This is line 3.
```

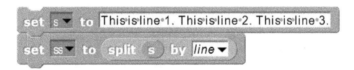

As you can guess, the variable 'ss' will contain a list of 3 strings (i.e. the 3 lines).

This is how you can do this in **Python**:

```
s = "This is line 1.\nThis is line 2.\nThis is line 3."
ss = s.split('\n')
```

'\n' denotes the end-of-line character. Note that variable 's' could have got its content from a file read operation, which we will not cover in this book, because **Snap** does not bother with files. ☐

After running the script, the list 'ss' would contain the 3 lines as expected.

```
['This is line 1.', 'This is line 2.', 'This is line 3.']
```

Splitting at custom separator:
The **Snap** 'split' operator allows you to use your own separator (which can be a single letter) to split a long string into sub-strings.

The following example shows how you can take a line from a CSV (comma separated values) file and split it into words.

As you might expect, after running the script, ss will contain a list of 8 words.

Here is how the **Python** split() function can do this same thing for you:

```
s = "this,is,a,comma,separated,list,of,words"
ss = s.split(',')
```

After running the script, ss will contain a list of 8 words:

```
['this', 'is', 'a', 'comma', 'separated', 'list', 'of', 'words']
```

Character encoding:

Every alphanumeric letter is actually represented internally (in the computer memory) by an integer. The old ASCII standard used the range from 0 to 127 to represent all characters that you could enter using a standard English PC keyboard. Later, the Unicode standard came along, and it included letters from most world languages in addition to English.

Snap provides a way to work with this idea of "character encoding". The 'unicode of' operator gives you the underlying integer representation of the given letter. See examples below. The bubbles indicate the return value.

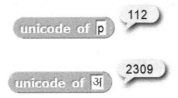

Conversely, the 'unicode' operator takes a number and tells us which letter (in Unicode) that number corresponds to. See examples below.

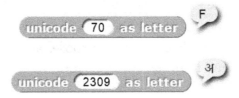

Python offers similar functionality through the functions chr() and ord().

The following script will display the encoding for letters H and w.

```
s = "Hello world!"
print( ord(s[0]), ord(s[6]) )
```

And the following script will display the letters corresponding to 70 and 2309.

```
print( chr(70), chr(2309) )
```

Note: An interesting and useful fact about character encoding is that the encodings of letters 'A' thru 'Z' and 'a' thru 'z' are contiguous. You can verify this yourself by printing their encodings.

String or number:

We often need to know if a string contains only numerals. In other words, does it represent an integer? **Snap** offers an operator that do this for us. See a few examples below. The bubbles indicate the return values.

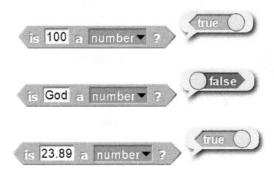

Python provides a string method for this purpose. `str.isdecimal()` checks if `str` contains an integer and returns `True` or `False`.

```
s = "Hello world!"
print( s.isdecimal() )
```

The above script will print `False`, whereas the script below will print `True`.

```
s = "250"
print( s.isdecimal() )
```

But, unlike **Snap**, there is no function in **Python** (that I know of) to detect if a string contains a floating-point number, such as, 10.5, -200.2, etc.

The str() function:

The `str()` function converts other data types to string. See examples below:

```
s1 = str( 100 )
s2 = str( 234.56 )
print( s1 + s2 )
```

The print statement works only because s1 and s2 are both strings.

String slicing:

This is a technique of getting slices (substrings) of a given string.

`Syntax: string[ start : end : step ]`

It returns a substring from 'start' to 'end-1' separated by 'step'. Inputs 'end' and 'step' are optional.

Let us try string slicing on strings S1 and S2 as shown below.

```
S1 = 'usa'
S2 = "mexico's POPULATION is 20 m"
```

`S1[0]` gives "u".
`S2[3]` gives "i"
`S1[-1]` gives "a"
`S2[1:3]` gives "ex"
`S2[-4:-1]` gives "20 "

Blank 'start' is assumed to be 0.
`S2[:4]` gives 'mexi'
Blank 'end' includes the last character.
`S[1:]` gives 'sa'
`S1[:-1]` gives 'us'
Negative numbers work backwards.
`S2[5:3:-1]` gives 'oc'

Strings are immutable:

Unlike **Python** lists, strings are immutable, i.e., you cannot *modify* a string. The following (line 2) is not permitted:

```
S1 = "Abcde"
S1[0] = "a"
```

Random Numbers

Snap provides randomness in many different ways. The simplest is the following operator:

The range, as you know, can be changed. The following instruction picks a random number between -20 and 20 (both included).

And then, several other commands also offer the "random" flavor. Here are a few examples:

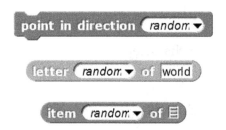

Actually, we can easily use the 'pick random' operator to create the same "random" effect in these and any other instructions in **Snap**. See the modified 'letter' operator below which does the exact same thing as its earlier flavor above:

Python comes with a library with a variety of "random" functions:

```
import random
```

And then, you can use the `random.randint()` function to achieve the exact same effect as the instruction shown earlier using **Snap's** 'pick random' operator.

```
n = random.randint(-20, 20)
```

Of course, the random library contains a lot of other useful functions, some of which are illustrated below.

`random()` returns a number between 0.0 and 1.0:
```
n = random.random()
```

`choice()` returns an element randomly from the given sequence. The first instruction below will return an item from the list, and the second instruction will pick a letter from the given string.

```
item = random.choice( ['abc', 'xyz', 50, -100] )
letter = random.choice( 'python' )
```

`sample(L,k)` returns a list of k randomly selected elements of the given sequence. The first instruction will pick 3 items at random, and the second instruction will pick 2 letters at random.

```
sublist = random.sample( [1,2,3,4,5], 3 )
letters = random.sample( "random string", 2 )
```

`shuffle()` shuffles the given list in place, i.e., it doesn't return anything.

```
L = [1,2,3,4,5]
random.shuffle(L)
```

List Data Structure

One of **Snap's** great strengths (compared to **Scratch**) is its substantially enhanced "list" capability. Interestingly, **Python's** own reputation is also partly due to its own "list" capability. And here is the good news: if you have a good understanding of **Snap's** list functionality, you can transfer that understanding to **Python** very easily.

Let's begin with the most basic **Snap** commands and their equivalent in **Python**. We will use the example of a list of fruits to illustrate various commands.

First, we create a list data structure:

Equivalent in **Python**:
```
fruits = []
```

Next, we add a few items:

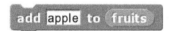

Equivalent in **Python**:
```
fruits.append( 'apple' )
```

After adding 'grape' and 'banana' in this way, let's insert 'kiwi' after 'apple':

Equivalent in **Python**:
```
fruits.insert( 1, 'kiwi' )
```

After all these operations, this is how the list will appear:
```
['apple', 'kiwi', 'grape', 'banana']
```

An important difference to note here is that **Snap** counts positions from 1, whereas **Python** counts from 0. So, 'apple' is at position 0, 'kiwi' is at 1, and so on.

Next, let us inspect a specific item in the list:

This would show 'grape'.

Equivalent in **Python**:
```
print( fruits[2] )
```

Let us find out the length of the list:

This would display 4.

Equivalent in **Python**:
```
print( len(fruits) )
```

Now, let us say we don't like kiwi so we will replace it with 'papaya':

Equivalent in **Python**:
```
fruits[1] = 'papaya'
```

Snap provides a condition to check if a certain item exists in a list:

Equivalent in **Python**:
```python
if 'papaya' in fruits:
    print( "There is at least one tropical fruit!" )
```

Okay, what if we want to remove an item from our list?

This command will remove 'grape' from the list.

Equivalent in **Python**:
```python
del fruits[2]
```

The 'del' command can in fact be used to delete multiple items.

The problem with the 'delete' block in **Snap** is that you need to know the position of the item you want to delete. What if you don't know it? **Snap** provides another interesting block that helps in this regard. You can use it to find the position of an item in the list:

The above script first finds out the location of 'banana' in the list and then uses 'delete' to remove it.

Equivalent in **Python**:

```
n = fruits.index( 'banana' )
del fruits[n]
```

Let us wrap up this section by discussing another very useful block in **Snap**, which you must have used often, to simply enumerate all items in a list.

This script will display the names of all fruits in the list one by one.

Equivalent in **Python**:
```
for item in fruits:
    print( item )
```

The **Python** list data structure offers a lot of interesting features through its class methods, such as, reverse(), pop(), count() and so on. You should explore these on your own. I will just discuss one very useful feature called slicing.

List slicing:
Syntax: string[start : end : step]
It returns a sub-list from start to end-1 separated by step. 'end' and 'step' are optional. Here are a few examples. We will use lists L1 and L2 to illustrate.

```
L1 = ['usa', 5, 6.7, 't']
L2 = [ 10, 'mexico', 10, 8, 4, 'a', -20, 45 ]
```

L2[1:3] gives ['mexico', 10]
L2[-4:-1] gives [4, 'a', -20]
Blank "start" is assumed to be 0.
L2[:4] gives [10, 'mexico', 10, 8]
Blank 'end' includes the last character.
L1[2:] gives [6.7, 't']
S1[:-1] gives 'us'

Pen Commands

Snap borrows the entire "Pen" capability (aka the Turtle feature) of **Scratch** and even enhances it a bit. **Python** does not have this capability built-in, but provides a library called the "Turtle" library which offers almost all the original Pen features of **Logo** (the very first Turtle language).

To use this library in **Python**, you need to import the Turtle library:

```
from turtle import *
```

I have provided a comprehensive list of Turtle commands in Appendix A. Here, we will just see the most important Pen commands in **Snap** and their equivalent in **Python**. See the table below:

clear	clearscreen()
pen down	pendown()
pen up	penup()
pen down?	isdown()
set pen color to	pencolor(), fillcolor(), color()
set pen size to	pensize()
fill	begin_fill(), end_fill()
write Hello! size 12	write()

Many of these commands such as, clearscreen() and penup() are easy to understand, but a few others may need further explanation.

The `isdown()` function returns `True` if the pen is down, `False` otherwise.

The **Python** color commands are a bit different from **Snap**. The `pencolor()` command lets you to set the pen color, `fillcolor()` lets you set the fill color, and `color()` lets you set both. Color can be specified in many ways, the most common being a string, such as, "red" or "purple". Several websites provide complete lists of available color names. Here is a colored chart format:

http://www.science.smith.edu/dftwiki/index.php/File:TkInterColorCharts.png

There is no equivalent to `change pen color by ○` in **Python**.

The `pensize()` command without any input returns the current pen size.

As a **Snap** programmer, you know that the actual drawing is done by **Snap's** motion commands. **Python's** "Turtle" library includes these motion commands. Appendix A gives a comprehensive list, but here is a quick sample:

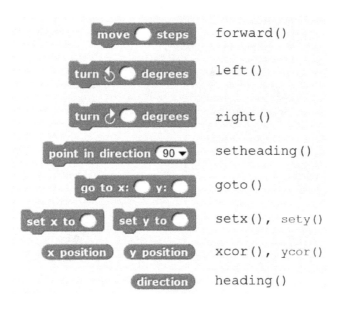

move ○ steps	`forward()`
turn ↺ ○ degrees	`left()`
turn ↻ ○ degrees	`right()`
point in direction (90 ▾)	`setheading()`
go to x: ○ y: ○	`goto()`
set x to ○ set y to ○	`setx()`, `sety()`
x position y position	`xcor()`, `ycor()`
direction	`heading()`

Section II

Practice Programs

Practice Program: Simple Calculator

Since the entire theme of this book is to transfer our **Snap** expertise to **Python**, we will do our practice programming by taking **Snap** programs and porting them to **Python**.

Let us begin with a **Snap** program that perform simple arithmetic operations.

Specification:

Write a simple calculator program that takes 2 numbers and performs basic arithmetic (add, subtract, divide, and multiply) on them. Provide a button for each operation.

Design:

Using 3 variables: 2 (x and y) for input and 1 (result) for output, we can manage all calculations. The click buttons will perform the actual calculation and the sprite will announce the result. Broadcasting will take care of all communication. Here is how the screen of my program looks like:

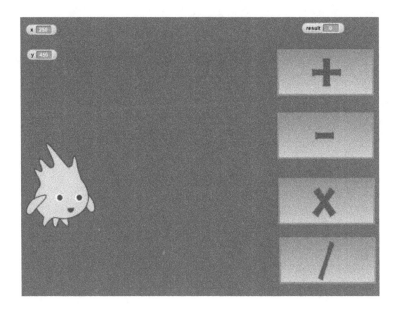

Snap program file:

You can compare your program with mine in the file below.

`Calculator.xml`

Python Version:

Since there is no broadcasting in **Python**, sending a broadcast will be implemented as a "function call". The "main" function will ask for the 2 input numbers and then go into a loop asking for the arithmetic operation to be performed, e.g. 'a' for add, 's' for subtract, and so on.

Python program file:

Compare your **Python** program with mine in the file below:

`Calculator.py`

Practice Program: Weights

There is a class or problems that involve using combinatorics, i.e. coming up with a collection of solutions for a single result. You will discover that you can write such programs quite easily in **Python**.

Specification:

Find all combinations for weights of 12, 20, and 30 kg such that their total is 300 kg. For example, 10 weights of 12 kg, 6 weights of 20 kg, and 2 weights of 30 kg add up to 300 kg.

Design hints:

Let's imagine we have to use only one weight – the 12 kg one.
How many 12 kg weights will make up 300?

Equation:
$12x = 300$
$x = 25$

Now, let's consider 3 weights:
How many combinations of 12, 20, and 30 kg weights can make up 300?

Equation:
$12x + 20y + 30z = 300$
Clearly, there are multiple combinations possible.

Here is a one-line algorithm to find all possible triplets:
`For every combination of (x, y, z) check if it meets the condition given in the equation.`

To do this we would basically need 3 nested simple loops – each for one of the weights. But what should their repeat counts be? The 12kg loop would go from 0 to 25 because beyond 25 the total value would exceed 300. We can calculate other loop counts in a similar fashion.

Snap program file:

You can compare your program with mine in the file below.

```
Weights.xml
```

Python version:

Now, using all the knowledge of **Python** we have gained so far, we will convert this program into a **Python** program.

Design hints:

This program will probably be just a single main function. There will be 3 nested loops that will try various combinations. The main concepts are: variables, looping, user input, and conditional statements.

Python program file:

Compare your solution with mine in the file below:

```
Weights.py
```

Practice Program: Circle Designs

Pen art is an exciting application of programming. Let us take up a **Snap** program that creates a few beautiful designs using circles.

Specification:

Using a basic procedure for "circle", draw the following shapes:

Design tips:

We will specify a "circle" procedure that you can use to draw all these different shapes. The procedure will take "diameter" as input.

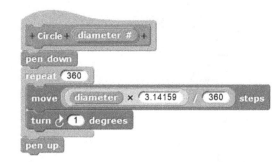

Diameter = Circumference / 3.14159

So, "circle 50" will draw a circle of diameter 50; "circle 150" will draw a circle of diameter 150; "circle 200" will draw a circle of diameter 200; and so on.

All the shapes shown above are various combinations of circles.

You can compare your program with mine in the file below.

`Circle-designs.xml.`

Python version:

Now, using all the knowledge of **Python** and the Turtle library we have gained so far, we will convert this program into a **Python** program.

We will first need to import the Turtle library.

Conversion of the procedures 'circle' and 'OlympicLogo' to **Python** functions should be straightforward. (Actually, you could directly use the circle() function of the Turtle library.) The 'earth' script which is invoked through a broadcast message will also become a **Python** function. There is no "turbo" mode in **Python**, but we can control speed through the speed() function.

You can compare your program with mine in the file below.

`Circle-designs.py`

Practice Program: Friends database

Let us now tackle a **Snap** program that manages a database of friends' names.

Specification:

Build a database of friends with click-buttons to add (a new friend), check (if a person is friend or not), remove (an existing friend), replace (an old one with a new one), count (the number of friends), and show (the entire list).

Design tips:

This program can be written using the "list" feature of **Snap**. There are list commands available to directly perform some of the database operations.

For example, the "add" command can be used to add new friends to the database. The "contains" condition can be used to check if a name already exists in the database. The "length of" operator can be used to find the number of friends.

The main challenge is figuring out how to "remove" and "replace" friends. There is no direct way to know where in the list a given name exists. For example, let's say you want to remove "Peter" from the database. You first need to find out where in the list "Peter" is located. Once you know the location number (e.g. 1, 2, etc.), you can use the "delete" command to remove "Peter" from the list.

The "index of" command allows you to "search" for a given name and return its position in the list.

Here is how the main screen of my Snap program looks like:

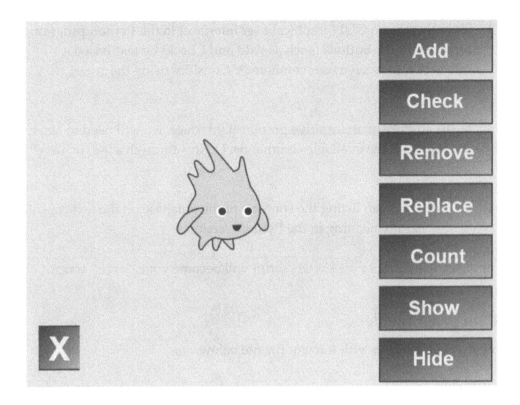

Snap program file:

You can compare your program with mine in the file below.

`Friends.xml`

Python version:

Now, using all the knowledge of **Python** we have gained so far, we will convert this program into a **Python** program.

Design hints:
1) Convert every **Snap** script into a separate **Python** function. For example, the script that receives the "add" broadcast message will become `addFriend()` function.

2) Since there is no GUI (graphical user interface) in the **Python** program, replace all click-buttons (such as Add and Check) by text-based interaction to receive user commands. Consider using the `input()` function.

3) In the absence of an intuitive graphical interface, we will need to assist the user with the available commands. Do this through a 'help' user input.

4) 'Show' will mean listing the contents of the database on the text console. 'Hide' has no meaning in the **Python** version.

5) The "Green flag clicked" script will become your "main" script.

Python program file:

Compare your solution with mine in the file below:

Friends.py

Practice Program: Recursive Squares

Recursion is an exciting idea in programming and Pen art is an excellent field where you can apply it. Here is one example.

Specification:

Design the following recursive drawing.

Design hints:

In recursive designs, the main challenge is to figure out the basic pattern which is repeated over and over again until a terminating condition is reached. In this case, we could use "depth of recursion" as the terminating condition.

The basic pattern in the given design (i.e. with no recursion) is a square. If you recurse another level, each existing square gets a "child" square (of half the parent's size) on top of each of its edges.

Thus, you could simply use an IF command to check the depth of recursion which would be passed as a parameter. If the depth is 0, only the basic pattern is drawn. If the depth is 1, the program will recurse once. And so on.

Recursing would involve getting in position to draw a smaller square on each edge and then making a self-call with a reduced depth and reduced square size.

Snap program file:

You can compare your program with mine in the file below.

`RecursiveSquares.xml`

Python version:

Now, using all the knowledge of **Python** we have gained so far, we will convert this program into a **Python** program.

The main concepts are: recursion, variables, looping, pen commands, and conditional statements.

Python program file:

Compare your solution with mine in the file below:

`RecursiveSquares.py`

Practice Program: Secret Number

Specification:

This is a 2-player game in which the human player picks a number between 1 and N and the computer tries to guess it in multiple attempts. The player decides N – the upper limit of the range of possible numbers from which the secret number is chosen.

The program keeps track of how many guesses computer has made and declares at the end. The human player helps by telling the computer whether the guessed number is correct, high, or low. The computer guesses using random guessing (but within the revised range after every guess).

Design hints:

Ask the user to guess the number in a forever loop. If the guess is correct, stop the script.

Here is the algorithm outline:

```
N = <ask user>
max = N, min = 0
guess = pick random between min and max
Ask user about guess
If guess = user number
      Declare win, attempts
      stop program
If guess > user number
      adjust max
Else
      adjust min
End if
Guess again ...
```

Snap program file:

You can compare your program with mine in the file below.

`Guessnumber.xml`

Python version:

Now, using all the knowledge of **Python** we have gained so far, we will convert this program into a **Python** program.

Design hints:

This program will probably be just a single main function. There will be a loop that continuously makes a guess and asks user to evaluate the guess. The main concepts are: variables, user input, and conditional statements.

Python program file:

Compare your solution with mine in the file below:

`Guessnumber.py`

Section III

Appendix

Appendix A: Python Turtle Primitives

Turtle procedures with no input and no output:

Name / shortcut	Operation
clearscreen	Clears screen; Turtle goes home, pen goes down. Background color becomes white and Turtle hides
home	Go to x=0, y=0
clear	Clears screen; Turtle doesn't move
penup / pu	Retract the pen. Future movements will not draw anything.
pendown / pd	Put the pen down. Future movements will start drawing.
hideturtle / ht	Hide the Turtle. Drawing is not affected.
showturtle / st	Show the Turtle.
begin_fill, end_fill	When end_fill() is called, the shape drawn after the last call to begin_fill() is filled.

Turtle procedures with input but no output:

Name / shortcut	Operation
forward / fd (N)	Move forward N steps
back / bk (N)	Move backward N steps
setx / sety (N)	Set X or Y coordinate of the Turtle to N
goto / setposition / setpos (X, Y)	Go to X, Y
left / lt (N)	Turn left. N is in degrees
right / rt (N)	Turn right. N is in degrees
setheading(N)	Make Turtle point at N degrees. In Python, East is 0, North is 90, …
color / pencolor / fillcolor ("color")	Set pen and/or fill color. Python takes color name ("red")
bgcolor ("color")	Set the background color.
pensize / width (N)	Set pen size to N. Default is 1.
circle (r, extent=None, steps=None)	Draw a circle of radius "r". Extent is in degrees. For 180 we get a semi-circle. If "r" is negative, draw clockwise. "steps" specifies # of edges of this polygon. Step=4 will draw a square!
write(text, move=False, align="left", font=("Arial",8,"normal"))	Write the given text using the specified font
screensize(w, h)	Set the screen size to width=w, height=h. If no arguments given it returns the current size.

Basic Procedures:

Name	Operation
bye ()	Exit Turtle library

Reporters and other procedures:

Name	Operation
speed()	Returns the current Turtle drawing speed.
speed(N)	Sets the Turtle's speed. N can be 0 to 10. If N is out of range it is taken as 0.
dot(d, color)	Draws a circular dot of diameter "d", filled with "color".
pensize()	Return current pen size
color/pencolor/fillcolor()	Return current color settings.
isdown()	True/False if pen down/up
xcor(), ycor()	Return Turtle's current X and Y coordinates
heading()	Return Turtle's current direction. East=0, North=90, West=180, South=270.

Color

Several commands above use a "color" argument. We have said above that this can be a string, such as, "red" or "green". But there are alternate ways to specify color.

```
# Use RGB values
colormode(255)
pencolor(40, 100, 255)
```

Speeding up drawing

Even with the highest speed (see speed() command above), the drawing can get slow for complex drawings, such as, recursive designs. You can speed up even further by using the tracer() and update() functions, which work somewhat like the "turbo" feature in **Snap** (which turns on/off the animation).

This code turns off animation completely, so the drawing is visible only at the very end.

```
tracer(0, 0)
# Code to draw your design
update()
```

This code makes animation run intermittently, so the drawing updates are visible less frequently. '5' below means refresh display only every 5th time.

```
tracer(5, 0)
# Code to draw your design
update()
```

Slowing down drawing

For whatever reason (maybe debugging) If you want slower speeds even than the lowest speed offered by speed() command above, you can use the delay() command to slow down the animation.

```
# Every drawing sub-step is delayed by 200 ms
delay(200)
# Code to draw your design
```

www.ingramcontent.com/pod-product-compliance
Lightning Source LLC
Chambersburg PA
CBHW060204060326
40690CB00018B/4242